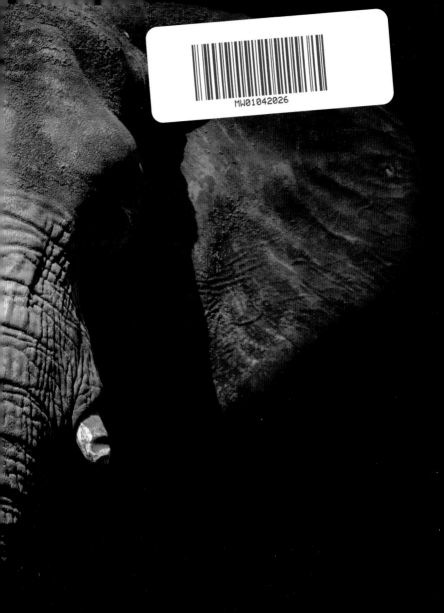
MW01042026

WISDOM
of
ELEPHANTS

MOSELEY ROAD INC.
International Rights and Packaging
22 Knollwood Avenue
Elmsford, NY 10523
www.moseleyroad.com

President: Sean Moore
Editor: Finn Moore
Art director and photo research: Grace Moore
Printed in China

ISBN 978-1-62669-149-0

WISDOM
— of —
ELEPHANTS

Compiled by
Grace Moore

mri

Moseley Road, Inc.
Elmsford, New York

"I don't think what size I am really matters."

- JOSE ALTUVE

"So long as the memory of certain beloved friends lives in my heart, I shall say that life is good."

- HELEN KELLER

"It's surprising how much memory is built around things unnoticed at the time."

- BARBARA KINGSOLVER

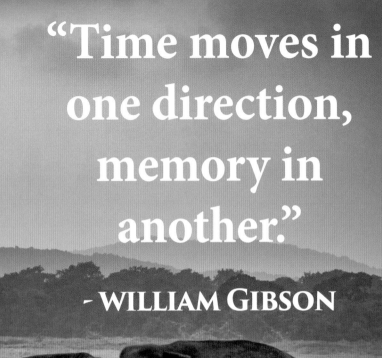

"Time moves in one direction, memory in another."

- WILLIAM GIBSON

"Those who love deeply never grow old; they may die of old age, but they die young."

- DOROTHY CANFIELD FISHER

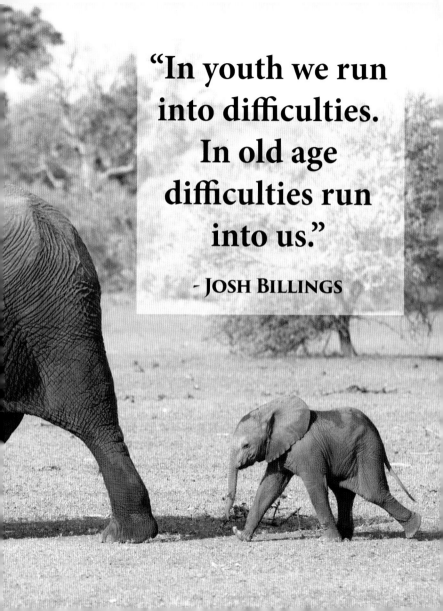

"In youth we run into difficulties. In old age difficulties run into us."

- JOSH BILLINGS

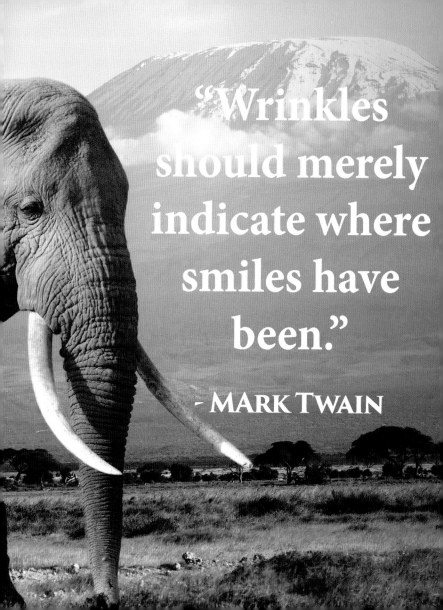

"Wrinkles should merely indicate where smiles have been."

- MARK TWAIN

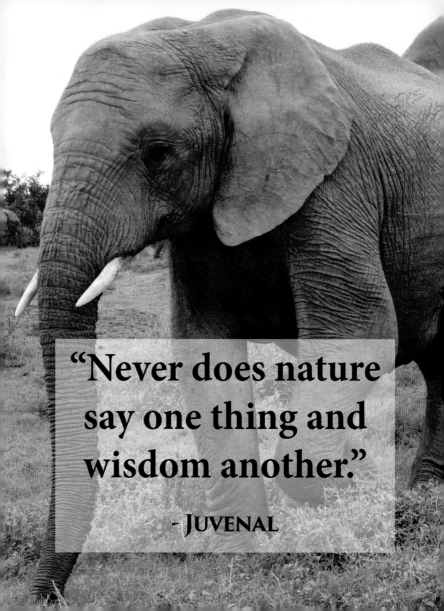

"Never does nature say one thing and wisdom another."

- JUVENAL

"The secret of genius is to carry the spirit of the child into old age, which means never losing your enthusiasm."

- ALDOUS HUXLEY

"If wrinkles must be written upon our brows, let them not be written upon the heart. The spirit should never grow old."

- JAMES A. GARFIELD

"Your self is created by your memories, and your memories are created by your mental habits. "

- RICK WARREN

"You can be whatever size you are, and you can be beautiful both inside and out. We're always told what's beautiful and what's not, and that's not right."

- SERENA WILLIAMS

"As you get older,
the pickings get
slimmer, but the
people don't."

- CARRIE FISHER

"Without memory, there is no culture.

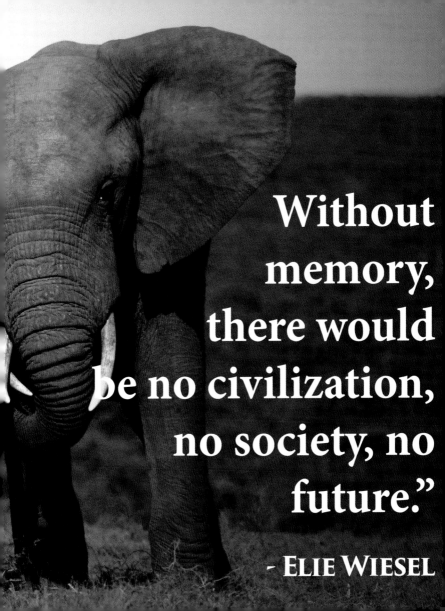

Without memory, there would be no civilization, no society, no future."

- ELIE WIESEL

"Time and memory are true artists; they remould reality nearer to the heart's desire."

- JOHN DEWEY

"It's not the size of the dreamer, it's the size of the dream."

- JOSH RYAN EVANS

"Memory... is the diary that we all carry about with us."

- OSCAR WILDE

"Anyone who stops learning is old, whether at twenty or eighty. Anyone who keeps learning stays young. The greatest thing in life is to keep your mind young."

- HENRY FORD

"Never cut a tree down in the wintertime. Never make a negative decision in the low time. Never make your most important decisions when you are in your worst moods.

Wait. Be patient.
The storm will pass.
The spring will come."

- ROBERT H. SCHULLER

"I am grateful for all the moments I have, and I'm moving forward one step at a time to the future."

- PARK BO-GUM

"True wisdom comes to each of us when we realize how little we understand about life, ourselves, and the world around us."

- SOCRATES

"Do not wait; the time will never be 'just right'. Start where you stand, and work with whatever tools you may have at your command, and better tools will be found as you go along."

- GEORGE HERBERT

"There are many ways of going forward,

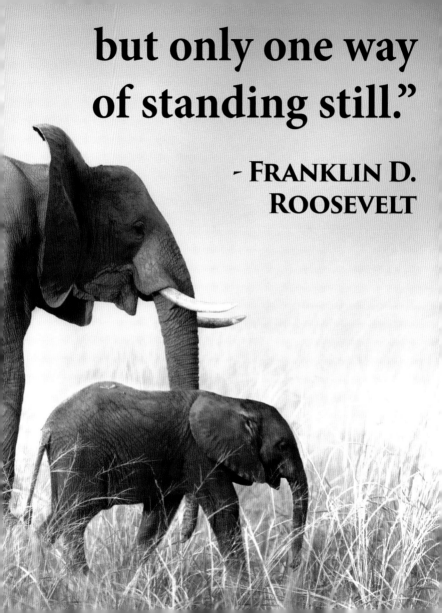

"In every walk
with nature

one receives far
more than he seeks."
- JOHN MUIR

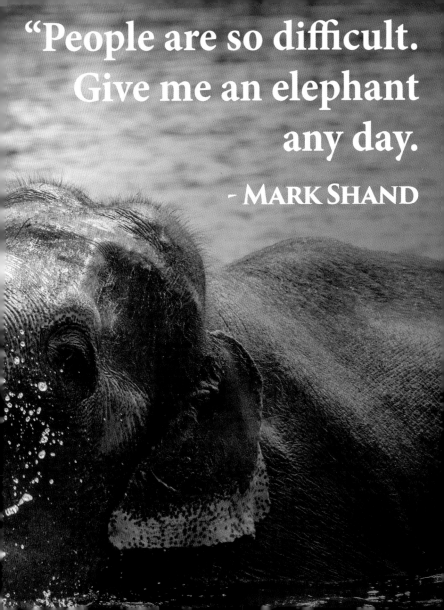

"Only the weak are cruel. Gentleness can only be expected from the strong."

- LEO BUSCAGLIA

"Wisdom begins in wonder."

- SOCRATES

"Nature's great masterpiece, an elephant; the only harmless great thing."

- JOHN DONNE

"What wisdom can you find that is greater than kindness?"

— JEAN-JACQUES ROUSSEAU

"I don't think about size — I focus more on being powerful and confident."

SIMONE BILES

"Don't gain the world
and lose your soul;

wisdom is better than silver or gold."
- BOB MARLEY

"I have just three things to teach: simplicity, patience, compassion. These three are your greatest treasures."

- BOB MARLEY

"Not by age but by capacity is wisdom acquired."

- PLAUTUS

"Growing old with someone else is beautiful, but growing old while being true to yourself is divine."

- DODINSKY

"In the end, it's not years in your life that count. It's the life in your years."

- ABRAHAM LINCOLN

"Nothing is miserable unless you think it so; and on the other hand, nothing brings happiness unless you are content with it."

- BOETHIUS

"Be happy in the moment, that's enough. Each moment is all we need, not more."

- MOTHER TERESA

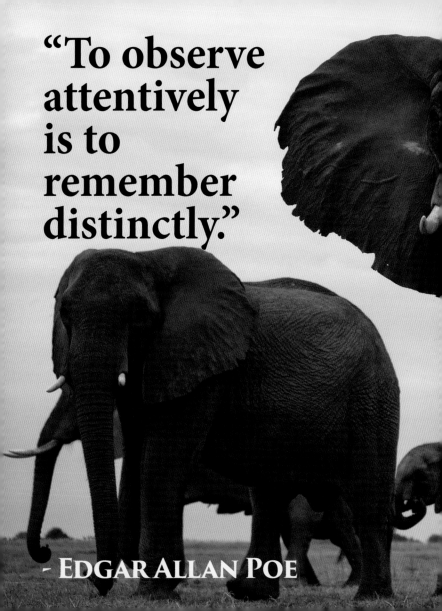

"To observe attentively is to remember distinctly."

- EDGAR ALLAN POE

"No one can ever take your memories from you — each day is a new beginning, make good memories every day."

- CATHERINE PULSIFER

"To me, beauty is inclusion — every size, every color — that's the world I live in."

- PRABAL GURUNG

"Science and technology revolutionize our lives, but memory, tradition and myth from our response."

- ARTHUR M. SCHLESINGER

"When grace is joined with wrinkles, it is adorable. There is an unspeakable dawn in happy old age."

- VICTOR HUGO

"The only true wisdom is knowing you know nothing."

- SOCRATES

"Kindness is more important than wisdom, and the recognition of this is the beginning of wisdom."

- THEODORE ISAAC RUBIN

"We are what our thoughts have made us; so take care about what you think. Words are secondary. Thoughts live; they travel far."

- SWAMI VIVEKANANDA

"By three methods we may learn wisdom: First, by reflection, which is noblest; Second, by imitation, which is easiest; and Third by experience, which is the bitterest."

- CONFUCIUS

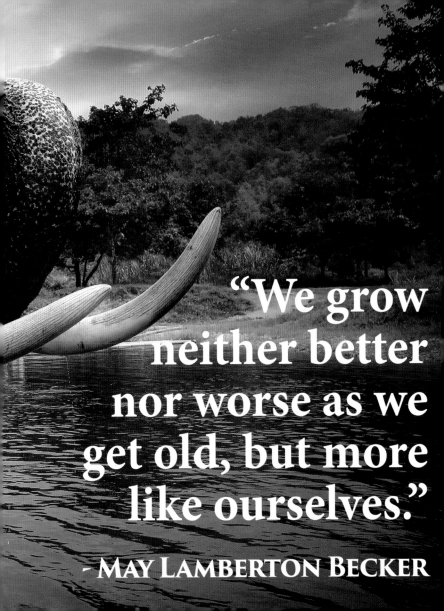

"We grow neither better nor worse as we get old, but more like ourselves."

- MAY LAMBERTON BECKER

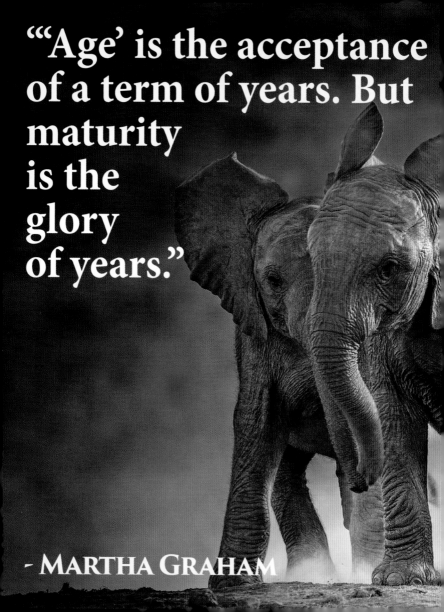

"I have just three things to teach: simplicity, patience, compassion. These three are your greatest treasures."

- LAO TZU

"A tree is known by its fruit; a man by his deeds. A good deed is never lost; he who sows courtesy reaps friendship, and he who plants kindness gathers love."

- SAINT BASIL

"Age appears to be best in four things; old wood best to burn, old wine to drink, old friends to trust, and old authors to read."

- FRANCIS BACON

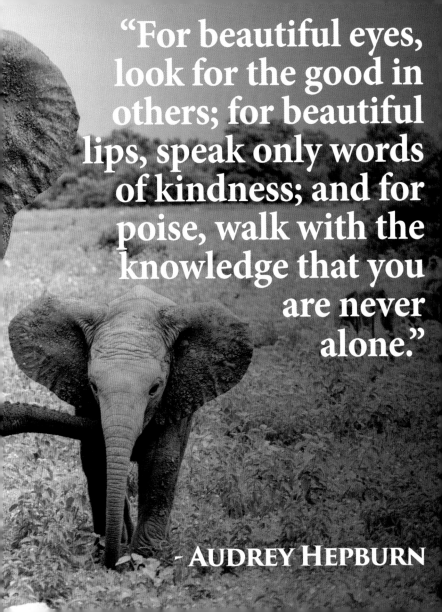

"With age comes a greater wisdom, an ease and comfort with oneself."

- CHERIE LUNGHI

PICTURE CREDITS

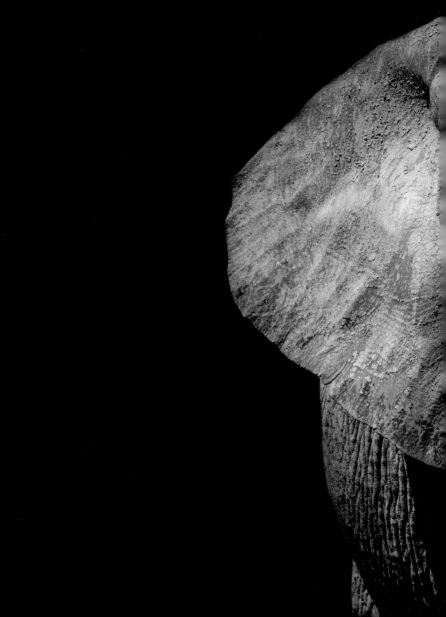